D1034985

A Closer Look at
PLANT REPRODUCTION, GROWTH, AND ECOLOGY

Published in 2012 by Britannica Educational Publishing
(a trademark of Encyclopædia Britannica, Inc.)
in association with Rosen Educational Services, LLC
29 East 21st Street, New York, NY 10010.

Distributed exclusively by Rosen Educational Services.
For a listing of additional Britannica Educational Publishing titles, call toll free (800) 237-9932.

First Edition

Britannica Educational Publishing
Michael I. Levy: Executive Editor, Encyclopædia Britannica
J.E. Luebering: Director, Core Reference Group, Encyclopædia Britannica
Adam Augustyn: Assistant Manager, Encyclopædia Britannica

Anthony L. Green: Editor, Compton's by Britannica
Michael Anderson: Senior Editor, Compton's by Britannica
Sherman Hollar: Associate Editor, Compton's by Britannica

Marilyn L. Barton: Senior Coordinator, Production Control
Steven Bosco: Director, Editorial Technologies
Lisa S. Braucher: Senior Producer and Data Editor
Yvette Charboneau: Senior Copy Editor
Kathy Nakamura: Manager, Media Acquisition

Rosen Educational Services
Jeanne Nagle: Senior Editor
Nelson Sá: Art Director
Cindy Reiman: Photography Manager
Karen Huang: Photo Researcher
Matthew Cauli: Designer, Cover Design
Introduction by Jeanne Nagle

Library of Congress Cataloging-in-Publication Data

A closer look at plant reproduction, growth, and ecology / edited by Michael Anderson. — 1st ed.
    p. cm. — (Introduction to biology)
"In association with Britannica Educational Publishing, Rosen Educational Services."
Includes bibliographical references and index.
ISBN 978-1-61530-530-8 (library binding)
1. Plants — Reproduction — Juvenile literature. 2. Growth (Plants) — Juvenile literature. 3. Plant
ecology — Juvenile literature. I. Anderson, Michael, 1972-
QK825.C53 2012
581.3 — dc22

                                                                              2011008271

Manufactured in the United States of America

Cover and interior background images Shutterstock.com

A Closer Look at

PLANT
REPRODUCTION
GROWTH, AND
ECOLOGY

Edited by Michael Anders

Britannica®
Educational Publishing
IN ASSOCIATION WITH

ROSEN
EDUCATIONAL SERVICES

CONTENTS

I n many ways, plants are like any other living organism. A plant is born, grows, develops, reproduces, and, like animals and humans, plays a vital role in sustaining the environment in which it lives. Yet there are also a number of life processes that set plants apart from other living things. As this book details, the habits and survival methods of plant life on Earth range from the simply curious to the truly remarkable.

Consider the ways in which plants reproduce. Some plants are created by the joining of one parent plant's male sex cells and another's female sex cells. Humans and most animals also reproduce in this way. Yet there are other methods of plant reproduction that don't depend upon two parents, or even sex cells, for that matter. Leaves and stems—whether they break off on their own, are cut on purpose, or naturally grow underground (in the case of tubers and bulbs)—are capable of sprouting roots and "giving birth" to a new, independent plant.

All living things depend on water for their survival. This is especially true of plants. The role of water in the life of a plant is a lot like that of blood in humans and animals; water carries nutrients and other molecules that keep plants alive. There is no organ like a heart, though, to move water through a plant's system. Instead, plants rely on transpiration and diffusion.

Transpiration is the process that allows water to reach all the cells throughout a plant. Plants constantly lose water by "sweating" through tiny openings in their leaves. This causes lower water concentrations in leaf cells. The plant responds by drawing water from the soil into the roots and then up the stem to the leaves. Once water reaches a cell, it is drawn into the cell through diffusion. The interiors of plant cells have high levels of salt and sugars. In diffusion, water molecules move from where they are plentiful, outside cell membranes, to where they are in short supply, inside the cells.

No discussion of plant life would be complete without mention of photosynthesis. This is the process by which plants use sunlight, carbon dioxide, water, and minerals to create their own food. Photosynthesis also benefits other living creatures, including humans. For one thing, any organism that eats plants absorbs the nutrients that photosynthesis creates. The benefits extend to other creatures that eat plant-eaters in what

is known as a food chain. Also as the result of photosynthesis, plants release oxygen into the atmosphere. Humans and many other living organisms need oxygen to live.

Plants also play an important part in developing ecosystems, or natural environments. Dead leaves, stems, and roots of plants leave their nutrients in soil, which makes it richer. The richer the soil, the more plants that are capable of growing there, and the more robust the ecosystem can become.

Animals typically don't care much about vegetation except as a food source. Likewise, people might overlook a blooming flower or a young tree as they go about their day. But the truth is that the life of a plant is valuable and wondrous, worthy of careful consideration.

Lavender blooms at the foot of a tree in Provence, France. **Shutterstock.com**

CHAPTER 1

METHODS OF PLANT REPRODUCTION

Plants continue to live on Earth by producing new plants. This process, called reproduction, may be sexual or asexual. Sexual reproduction involves the union of two different sex cells, while asexual reproduction occurs without a union of sex cells.

ASEXUAL REPRODUCTION

There are various types of asexual reproduction. Mosses and liverworts, for example, often contain plant fragments called gemmae in cuplike structures on their leaves or stems. Gemmae break loose and can germinate, or sprout, to establish a new plant, which is genetically identical to its parent.

Most vascular plants—that is, plants with specialized tissues for carrying water and food—can reproduce by a form of asexual reproduction known as vegetative reproduction. For example, under the proper conditions, pieces of leaf or stem broken from a plant may produce roots and establish a new individual. Plants that produce

Some plants, such as strawberries, reproduce by growing offshoot plant stems called runners. Shutterstock.com

runners and stolons often reproduce vegetatively. Runners are stems that run along the ground, and stolons are stems that grow erect and then curve over, touching the ground at the tip. The strawberry produces runners that may establish a new plant. The runners can then be broken without disturbing the parent or the new plant.

Many garden plants reproduce more efficiently from roots, stems, and leaves than from seeds (which are a part of sexual reproduction). Such vegetative reproduction has the advantage of producing larger plants more rapidly. The potato seed, for example, is very small and develops into a small, weak plant. The potato itself, though, is actually a tuber—a fleshy underground stem—that contains a reserve supply of starch and produces a strong, fast-growing plant. Vegetative reproduction enables plants to spread quickly over the area surrounding the parent plant. Many weeds are difficult to control because they grow quickly using vegetative reproduction. In addition to runners and tubers, bulbs (underground buds), corms (vertical underground stems), and rhizomes (horizontal underground stems) are other parts from which new plants may grow.

Cuttings, also called slips, are twigs, branches, or leaves cut from the parent plant and placed in soil, sand, or water. In time, new roots, stems, and leaves grow from the cuttings. The willow tree, geranium, begonia, and African violet are examples of plants that may be produced in this way. A process called layering is used with certain trees and shrubs. When a branch is bent down to touch the soil, it sends roots into the ground and a new plant results. Gooseberries, blackberries, grapevines, and forsythia may be reproduced in this way.

Improved varieties of fruit are obtained by grafting. In this process the stem of a plant that has produced superior fruit is made to grow on the stem of another plant, called the stock, of hardy but inferior quality. The stems are cut so that the cambium layers (a type of growth tissue) of the two are in contact and grow together. The cuts are then tied together and covered with cloth or with a special wax. Budding is the process of removing a bud from one plant and setting it into the bark of another, usually a young seedling.

SEXUAL REPRODUCTION

In sexual reproduction, male and female cells, called gametes, unite to form a single cell, called a zygote. This zygote then undergoes cell division, ultimately giving rise to a new plant body. Offspring produced by asexual reproduction are identical to their parent. Offspring produced sexually, however, have two parents and so, though they certainly resemble the parents, the offspring are not necessarily identical to them. Consequently,

sexual reproduction is a process that increases variation among offspring.

ALTERNATION OF GENERATIONS

In plants, the process of sexual reproduction takes place in two distinct phases, or generations. In one phase the organism reproduces by means of spores and in the other by means of sex cells. This reproductive pattern is called alternation of generations.

The structure that produces spores is known as the sporophyte. Spores are single cells that, like the gametes of animals, are produced by a type of cell division called meiosis. When a spore germinates, it produces the gametophyte, the structure that produces gametes. When a male gamete, or sperm, unites with a female gamete, or egg, they form the zygote.

The alternation of generations is perhaps most clearly seen in ferns, because the sporophyte and gametophyte form independent structures. The common fern fronds that grow along stream banks are sporophytes. They produce spores in structures called sori, which are often found on the underside of the plant's leaves. When a released spore lands at a place favorable for germination, it grows

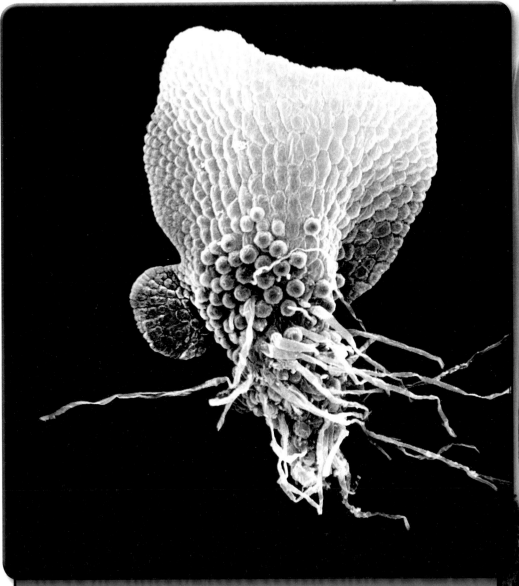

A fern gametophyte. The gametophytes of sexually reproducing plants are responsible for the production of gametes, which each contain one complete set of chromosomes. **Dr. Richard Kessel & Dr. Gene Shih/ Visuals Unlimited/Getty Images**

into the gametophyte. The gametophyte is a heart-shaped plant less than 0.25 inches (0.6 cm) across and it produces male and female gametes. When a male gamete unites with a female gamete, a zygote is formed that grows into a young fern plant—another sporophyte. Ferns most often grow in moist habitats, such as along streams, because the male gametes require moisture in order to move to the location of the female gametes.

REPRODUCTION IN SEED PLANTS

The most highly developed plants are those that produce new plants by means of seeds. In seed plants, the dominant form of the plant is the sporophyte. The gametophytes are usually microscopic and form within a part of the sporophyte, typically a cone or flower. Seeds then develop from the union of a male and a female cell produced by the gametophytes. The development of reproduction by means of seeds allowed plants to propagate in many different habitats. For example, unlike ferns, seed plants can reproduce even in very dry locations.

The earliest seed plants were seed ferns, which are now extinct. They produced their seeds on special leaves. Then the conifers

The seeds of pine trees are contained within the scales of pinecones. Fertilized seeds drop from the scales and produce new trees, or seedlings, where they fall. Shutterstock.com

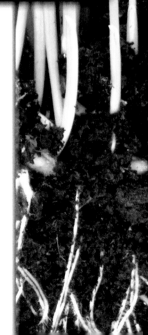

and their relatives evolved. These plants produce sex cells on the scales of cones. The male sex cells are produced in small cones called microstroboli. During pollination, billions of pollen grains, which produce sperm, are released from these cones into the wind. Most of this pollen falls to the ground and is wasted, but a small amount of the pollen

17

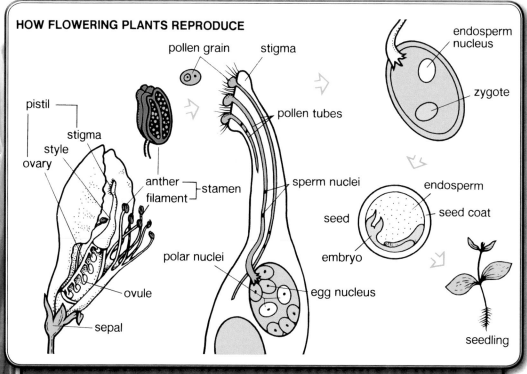

HOW FLOWERING PLANTS REPRODUCE

A diagram showing the pollination process of flowering plants.
Encyclopedia Britannica, Inc.

produced lodges on the ovules of the female cones. The ovules contain the egg cells. The pollen grains germinate and produce a pollen tube that carries the sperm to the egg. The egg and sperm unite to form a zygote. The zygote then divides by normal cell division to produce an embryonic plant. The embryo and the ovule that surround it together form the seed.

SELF-POLLINATION VS. CROSS-POLLINATION

Some flowers are self-pollinating; that is, their eggs can be fertilized by sperm that come from their own pollen. In most cases, however, nature takes great care to prevent self-pollination because cross-pollination usually produces plants that are stronger and healthier. This requires the transfer of pollen from one plant to the stigma of another plant of the same species.

Cross-pollination clearly has evolutionary advantages for the species. The seeds formed may combine the hereditary traits of both parents, and the resulting offspring generally are more varied than would be the case after self-pollination. In a changing environment, the plants resulting from cross-pollination are typically better able to adapt to their new situation, ensuring survival of the species.

Flowers avoid self-pollination in several ways. In some cases the stamens and pistils mature at different times. In other flowers the stamens are shorter than the pistils and hence do not deposit pollen on their own stigma. Wind-pollinated flowers usually bear the stamens and pistils in separate flowers. Alders, birches, walnuts, and hickories bear catkins—clusters of unisex flowers—with pistillate flowers on some branches and catkins with staminate flowers on other branches. Corn has the pistils and stamens on different parts of the same plant. The tassel bears the staminate flowers and the ear bears the pistillate flowers. These are known as monoecious (of the same household) plants. A few trees, such as cottonwoods and willows, carry the separation even further, with the staminate flowers on one tree and the pistillate on another. These are known as dioecious (of two households) plants.

Tassels on an ear of corn. **Shutterstock.com**

Pollination in the flowering plants is far more efficient. The brilliant colors, delicate perfumes, and sweet nectar of many flowering plants attract insect visitors to the flowers. Pollen from the flower's stamen is picked up by the hairs on the insects' bodies and carried to another flower. Some of these pollen grains then rub off the insect and onto the top of the flower's pistil, called the stigma. These pollen grains then germinate, producing a pollen tube that carries sperm cells to the egg within the ovules in the ovary. Two sperm nuclei then pass through the pollen tube. One of them unites with the egg nucleus and produces a zygote. The other sperm nucleus unites with two other nuclei, called polar nuclei, to produce a structure that develops into the endosperm, which provides nutrients for the growing plant. The embryo and ovule develop to form the seed and the ovary becomes the fruit.

CHAPTER 2

PLANT GROWTH AND DEVELOPMENT

The growth of a plant begins with the germination of a seed. From the moment that the seed coat breaks and the roots begin to emerge, the young plant undergoes a number of processes that are essential to its survival. Diffusion, for example, brings water from the soil into the plant's roots. Photosynthesis allows the plant to use sunlight to make its own food. And respiration uses some of the food produced during photosynthesis to create energy, which the plant needs to carry on all of the activities necessary for life.

SEED GERMINATION

The embryo has all of the basic plant parts. As the seed begins to grow, its epicotyl or plumule—the new plant's first bud—will form the plant shoot. The cotyledons quickly unfold into leaves and begin producing food for the plant. The radicle gives rise to the root system. The region that connects the radicle and plumule is called the hypocotyl.

Coconuts are seeds of the coconut palm. The white meat and "milk" inside a coconut are the endosperm, which provides nutrition for the embryonic plant that grows when the seed is fertilized. Shutterstock.com

In most plants, the nutritive tissue in the seed is endosperm, formed during the fertilization process. Seeds with large amounts of endosperm include those of corn, castor beans, and pumpkins. The "milk" contained in coconuts is actually endosperm. The seeds of other plants, such as beans and peas, contain very little endosperm. In these plants the cotyledons of the embryo

are quite large and provide nourishment to the embryo during germination.

Seed germination requires moisture, oxygen, and a suitable temperature, but there are sufficient food and minerals stored in the seed so that these factors are not necessarily essential during the very early stages of germination. Many seeds germinate best in the dark. Initially they can grow using food reserves from the endosperm or cotyledons. Within a few days of germination, however, the developing seedling must have light in order to manufacture its own food.

BIRTH OF A PLANT

Seed germination begins when the seed absorbs water. This causes the inner tissue layers to swell enough to rupture the seed coat. Water also hastens chemical reactions that occur very slowly in dormant dry seeds. These chemical reactions provide food directly to the embryo, causing it to begin its growth.

The rapid growth of the embryo results in very high rates of respiration. This is why oxygen is so important for the germination of most seeds. Seeds that are deprived of

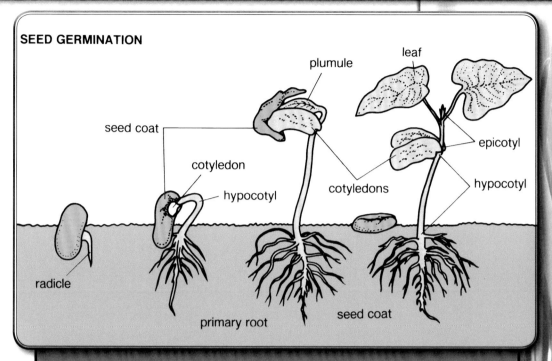

A diagram depicting the germination of a bean seed. **Encyclopædia Britannica, Inc.**

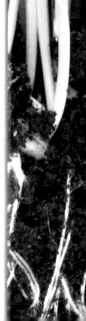

oxygen once they begin to germinate soon die. This sometimes happens when planted seeds receive too much water—oxygen cannot diffuse easily into very wet soil.

Once germination of the seed begins, the radicle emerges. The radicle grows rapidly downward through the soil to establish the root system. In some plants, such as beans, the tissues that make up the hypocotyl

stretch, pushing the cotyledons above the soil. The cotyledons can then unfold and begin producing food. In plants with cotyledons that store food, the cotyledons may remain in the soil. Once the root system is established, the epicotyl rapidly develops into a system of shoots and leaves.

DORMANCY

Before germination, dry seeds are very resistant to environmental stresses such as drought or unfavorable temperatures. This portion of the plant's life cycle allows the plant to survive during periods when plant growth is impossible. In order to prevent germination when conditions are unfavorable, many seeds are dormant when they are produced. This means that they will not germinate even if there is sufficient moisture and oxygen and suitable temperatures. Such seeds are nevertheless alive. If allowed to "afterripen" for a period of weeks or months, they will germinate normally.

Many plants that grow in cold winter regions produce dormant seeds. Such seeds germinate in the spring, often only after they have been exposed to cold, moist conditions.

Purple crocuses blooming amid the snowy remnant of winter. Crocuses are dormant until late winter and early spring, when ground and air temperatures are favorable for germination. Shutterstock.com

SPECIAL CONDITIONS

Some seeds require special conditions to germinate. Such requirements often guarantee that the seed will germinate only when conditions are most favorable for seedling growth. Seeds of the pin cherry, for example, may remain dormant in forest soils for decades.

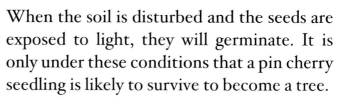

Greenery and blossoms grow amid the charred remains of California scrubland after a fire. Some plant seeds are awakened from dormancy by the intense heat of wildfires. **Richard Herrmann/Visuals Unlimited/ Getty Images**

When the soil is disturbed and the seeds are exposed to light, they will germinate. It is only under these conditions that a pin cherry seedling is likely to survive to become a tree.

In desert regions the seeds of many plant species germinate only following very heavy rains, when sufficient moisture will be available for the plants to complete their life cycles. The seed coats of many such plants contain chemical inhibitors that prevent normal germination. Heavy rains remove these inhibitors, permitting germination. Other plants germinate and grow best in areas that have recently been burned by wildfire. The heat of the fire is the stimulus that breaks the seed's dormancy.

WATER MOVEMENT

Most plants require large quantities of water in order to grow and reproduce. Water is crucial for photosynthesis; it is the liquid in which all other molecules, including food and minerals, are transported through the plant. In addition, water pressure in plant cells, called turgor, is necessary for maintaining cell growth and plant structure.

Large quantities of water move through a plant each day. In plants there is no "pump" comparable to the heart in many animals that serves to move liquids. Instead, plants depend on other processes to move water through their bodies.

DIFFUSION

One such process is diffusion. This is the movement of water molecules from areas

of high concentration (areas with many water molecules) to areas of low concentration (areas with few water molecules). When diffusion occurs across a living membrane, it is called osmosis. Cell membranes are semipermeable—that is, some molecules, such as water, pass through them easily while other molecules, such as sugars and some salts, do not. The jelly-like substance inside the cell, called cytoplasm, contains large amounts of sugars and salts. When cells come in contact with water, the concentration of water is greater on the outside of the cell than it is on the inside. The difference in

Water pressure, or turgor (expansion) stimulate plant cell growth. A lack of water not only stops growth but can cause plants to wilt and eventually die. Shutterstock.com

concentrations causes water to diffuse into the cell. This is how water moves from the soil into the cells of plant roots.

As more and more water diffuses into the cell, the turgor of the cell increases. Cell turgor is very important to plant growth and structure. Turgor causes expansion of the cell wall and stimulates cell growth. It also keeps cells rigid and so enables the plant to remain upright. Loss of water, and consequently of turgor, from plant cells causes the entire plant to wilt. This can happen when the soil becomes too dry. It can also happen when too much fertilizer is added to soil, because fertilizer increases the concentration of minerals in the soil. This decreases the concentration of water molecules. When this happens, even though the soil feels moist, water diffuses out of the plant cells and the plant wilts.

TRANSPIRATION

Once water enters a plant through the roots, it must be transported to other plant tissues. In the process known as transpiration, water is constantly evaporating from leaf cells—through the stomata (openings) of the leaves—and into the atmosphere. This is particularly true during the daytime when the

stomata are open and the air is warm. It is estimated that a single oak tree gives off 90 to 100 gallons (340 to 380 liters) of water each day.

Transpiration from the leaf cells lowers the concentration of water in these cells. This causes water to diffuse into the leaf cells from the cells of the xylem (a tissue that carries water and minerals) in the leaf veins. The loss of water from the xylem in the leaf veins lowers the concentration of water in the xylem tissues of the leaf. This causes water to move from the xylem of the stem into the leaves. Movement of water up the stem lowers the concentration of water molecules in the xylem of the root, causing water to be drawn from the root cells and so from the soil. Thus, water is pulled up the plant as a result of the transpiration from leaf surfaces.

Many plants that grow in hot, dry habitats have adaptations that decrease the rate of transpiration and so decrease the amount of water needed by the plants. For example, the cuticle, or outer layer, of the leaves of some plants is very thick. This waxy layer prevents excessive water loss from the leaves. Many succulent plants, such as the many species of cacti, are able to take up and store large quantities of water when it is abundant. They can then survive on this stored water during dry periods.

CACTI: THE IDEAL DESERT DWELLERS

The plants known as cacti are well suited for life in the desert. Their unique ability to store water allows them to flourish in arid conditions in which other plants could not survive.

Cacti are characterized by their adaptations to the harsh desert environment. In the process

A common succulent plant of the southwestern United States, the Engelmann prickly pear (Opuntia engelmannii) *is also used as an ornamental plant in gardens.* **Grant Heilman Photography**

of transpiration, ordinary nondesert plants take up water from the soil by means of their roots and give off water through their leaves. A cactus has no leaves or only very small ones that usually drop off as the plant matures. The cactus thus avoids a huge loss of water. The stem is fleshy and thick and can store a large amount of water. Its tough skin keeps the water safely hoarded. Photosynthesis occurs on the green surface of the stem.

Cactus roots do not extend deep into the soil like those of other plants. Instead, they spread out near the surface. This enables the plant to absorb water from a wide area during the infrequent, light rains that occur in the desert.

PHOTOSYNTHESIS

In the process of photosynthesis, green plants and some other organisms use sunlight to produce food and oxygen, without which humans and other animals could not live. Photosynthesis is carried out in choloroplasts, which are specialized structures in the cytoplasm. Chloroplasts contain a green chemical compound called chlorophyll and a vast array of proteins called enzymes. These enzymes are essential to the many reactions involved in photosynthesis.

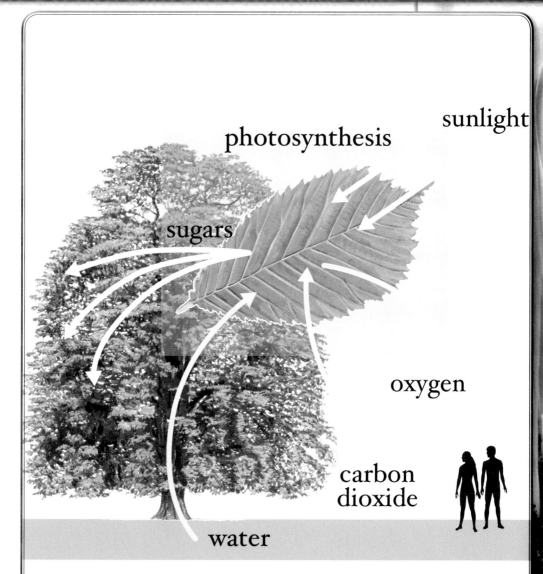

Diagram of photosynthesis showing how green plants capture sunlight and use it to transform water and carbon dioxide into oxygen and sugars. **Encyclopædia Britannica, Inc.**

Light energy is initially trapped by one of several chlorophyll pigments. Chlorophyll a is the most abundant of these pigments. Chlorophyll b is also found in most green tissues.

Carbon dioxide from the air enters the leaf through the stomata. Water travels to the leaf cells from the soil through the xylem in the roots and stems. The captured light energy is then used to break down the water into oxygen molecules and hydrogen atoms, and to join these hydrogen atoms to the carbon dioxide molecules to make sugar molecules. Six molecules of oxygen are produced as a waste product and are released into the air through the stomata.

The sugar molecule formed in this process is glucose, a simple sugar. Enormous numbers of such molecules are produced in every chloroplast during each second of sunlight. Some of the glucose produced during photosynthesis is used by the plant in the process of respiration to generate other forms of energy. Much of the glucose, however, is converted into other molecules. Some is converted into the sugar sucrose, which is refined from sugarcane and sugar beets to make table sugar. By combining glucose molecules into long chains, or polymers, plant cells form starch and cellulose. Much of the stored food in plants is in the form of starch, and cellulose is the main component of plant cell walls. Sugars, starch, and cellulose belong to a general class of organic molecules called carbohydrates. In many plants, food is stored in the form of lipids, or fats—high-energy molecules that contain less oxygen than do carbohydrates.

Plants also need proteins and nucleic acids in order to survive. These compounds are made by combining carbohydrates with other elements, such as nitrogen, sulfur, phosphorus, potassium, iron, calcium, and magnesium. The plant roots obtain these essential elements from the soil.

RESPIRATION

To make cellulose, to build new cells, to store a reserve food supply, and to carry on all other activities necessary for living and growing, a plant needs energy. Energy is obtained by "burning" some of the glucose produced during photosynthesis. Just as coal releases energy when it burns in the presence of oxygen, so glucose and oxygen combine to release energy. The glucose is not burned in a fire, as is the case in a coal furnace, but the

chemical process, known as respiration, is similar. Respiration goes on day and night in every cell in a plant.

The chemical reactions involved in respiration are the reverse of those involved in photosynthesis. Oxygen combines with glucose to produce carbon dioxide and water and to release energy. Oxygen enters the plant through the stomata of the leaves, through the roots (either from air spaces in the soil or in solution in water), and through the air openings in the stems. Glucose combines with the oxygen to form carbon dioxide and water. The glucose is thus turned back into the same two substances from which it was made during photosynthesis, and the carbon dioxide and water vapor are released back into the air through the stomata. During the daytime, photosynthesis proceeds more rapidly than does respiration. As a result, plants release more oxygen than carbon dioxide and water vapor. At night, when photosynthesis stops (because of the absence of light), only oxygen is taken in, and carbon dioxide is given off as a waste product.

CHAPTER 3

INFLUENCES ON PLANT GROWTH

Plant growth and development are consequences of three processes: cell division (the process called mitosis), cell enlargement, and cell differentiation. Cell division in the meristem tissues at the tips of roots and shoot tips is primarily responsible for increases in the length of these plant parts. Cell division in the cambium tissues of the roots and stems causes these plant parts to increase in diameter.

Depending on where cell division takes place, a plant might grow lengthy, like the climbing plant at right, or expand in diameter, like the plant in the center pot. Peter Anderson/Dorling Kindersley/Getty Images

Much plant growth also results from cell enlargement. Plant cells can increase in size because their walls are elastic. As cells mature, they may then differentiate into specialized types of cells, such as fibers. The speed with which these processes of cell division, enlargement, and differentiation proceed is influenced by a number of factors, including environmental conditions, the presence of substances known as growth regulators, and heredity factors.

ENVIRONMENT AND NUTRIENTS

The rate of growth of a plant is directly related to the amount of food that the plant is able to produce. Consequently, plants grow best in environments that are favorable for photosynthesis. The availability of water also affects plant growth because water pressure inside the plant's cells provides the force necessary for cell enlargement. Plants grow more slowly when water is in short supply. If the environment becomes too dry, the pressure in the plant's cells may become so low that the plant wilts.

Plant growth is also influenced by other environmental factors. These include

Some plants, such as cacti and other desert plants thrive in hot, arid conditions that would be the ruin of other types of vegetation. However, the growth of these plants is quite slow. **David McNew/ Getty Images**

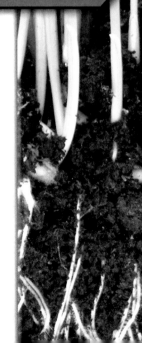

temperature and the availability of mineral nutrients such as nitrogen and phosphorus.

GROWTH REGULATORS

In addition to light, carbon dioxide, water, and minerals, plants need certain substances

in order to grow. These substances are called growth regulators, or hormones. They are produced in plants in very small quantities.

AUXINS

The first growth regulators to be discovered were the auxins. The term auxin comes from a Greek word meaning "to increase." The role that auxins play in the growth of plants was first demonstrated between 1926 and 1928 by the Dutch plant physiologist Frits W. Went. They play a key role in the growth of roots, stems, and buds and in the development of fruit.

Auxins are produced at the tips of stems and roots. They diffuse back to the growing cells of leaves, stems, and roots and stimulate these cells to grow longer. This function of auxins was proved when botanists stopped the growth of oat seedlings by cutting off the tips of the plants. Growth started again when juice from the tips was rubbed into the cut ends of the plant.

Auxins play a central role in plant-growth patterns called tropisms. Phototropism (meaning "light turning") is the growth of plants toward light. If a plant is exposed to

When gardeners prune bushes, trees, and hedges, they remove auxins, which are growth regulators produced at the tips of the plants' stems. Removal of auxins hinders plant growth. Shutterstock.com

light coming from a certain direction, the plant will bend in the direction of the light. This response is the result of the diffusion of auxins to the unlighted side of the plant, speeding up growth on that side and slowing down growth on the lighted side.

Geotropism (meaning "earth turning") is the growth of plant parts toward or away from a source of gravity—stems grow up and roots grow down. If a stem is laying sidewise, the force of gravity causes more auxins to accumulate on the lower surface of the stem. This accelerates the growth of the cells on the lower surface, causing the stem to bend upward. In plant roots, the accumulation of auxins on the lower surfaces causes the roots to grow down.

OTHER SUBSTANCES

Other growth regulators in plants include gibberellins, cytokinins, abscisic acid, and ethylene. Gibberellins promote the growth of stems and play a role in flowering, fruit production, and the breaking of dormancy in seeds and buds. Cytokinins promote cell division in roots and shoots and delay leaf senescence, such as the yellowing of leaves. Abscisic acid is a growth inhibitor. It causes

AUXINS AND BUDS

Gardeners have long known that if they remove the terminal bud at the tip of a plant's stem, the side buds develop and the plant becomes shorter and shrubbier. The reason is that the loss of the terminal bud stops the downward diffusion of auxins. As soon as the side buds develop enough auxins, they begin to grow and take over the task of checking the growth of the plant's lower buds. As long as the upper foliage and buds exposed to light are growing, the lower, shaded buds are arrested in their growth. The advantage to the plant is that if the upper buds and leaves are destroyed by frost, insects, or disease, the lower ones can then develop and take over the work of photosynthesis.

dormancy in seeds and buds and promotes the process that causes leaves to fall off a plant (abscission). Ethylene also promotes the abscission of leaves and promotes the ripening of a plant's fruit.

PHOTOPERIODISM

The rates of plant growth and cell differentiation vary from one season to the next. Plants are sensitive to the relative lengths

of alternating periods of darkness and light, which change with the seasons. This property is called photoperiodism. Depending on the seasonal lengths of day and night needed for blossoming, plants are divided into spring-, summer-, and fall-blossoming groups. Skunk cabbage, for example, is one of the earliest blooming spring plants in the northern United States. It requires longer nights than does the wild rose, which blooms three months later. Barley, wheat, and many other small grains blossom in early summer when the nights are relatively short, whereas corn, soybeans, and chrysanthemums bloom later, in midsummer and fall, when the nights are longer.

Plants actually "measure" the duration of darkness rather than of light. The photoperiodism of plants is caused by changes in a pigment called phytochrome (from two Greek words: *phyton*, meaning "plant," and *chroma*, meaning "color"). Phytochrome is a light-sensitive, blue-green pigment. It occurs in plant tissues in minute quantities—about one part in 10 million. The pigment acts

The growth regulator ethylene promotes the ripening of tomatoes and other plant fruit. Shutterstock.com

Chrysanthemums grow riotously in a field. Photoperiodism is a term that explains why some plants need extended daylight to grow while others, like chrysanthemums, bloom during the shorter days of autumn. Shutterstock.com

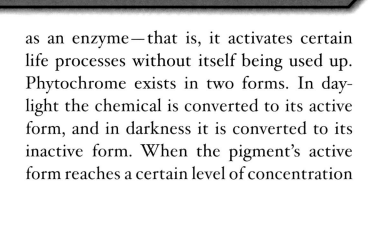

as an enzyme—that is, it activates certain life processes without itself being used up. Phytochrome exists in two forms. In daylight the chemical is converted to its active form, and in darkness it is converted to its inactive form. When the pigment's active form reaches a certain level of concentration

in the plant, it spurs changes in the plant's rate of growth.

Photoperiodism controls many plant growth processes other than flowering. Seed germination in many plants depends upon the amount and duration of light. The dormancy of trees and shrubs in winter is linked to the long nights of winter. In the laboratory, dormancy can be broken by shortening the period of darkness to which the plant is exposed. The buds then begin to develop.

CHAPTER 4

PLANT ECOLOGY

Plants are vital parts of nearly all terrestrial ecosystems. In ecosystems, energy is cycled through food chains. Plants trap light energy during photosynthesis and store it as chemical energy. That energy is then obtained by herbivores, which are organisms that eat plants and use the energy to grow and reproduce. Herbivores, in turn, are the primary energy source for carnivores—organisms that eat animals. In aquatic ecosystems, algae play a role similar to that of plants in terrestrial ecosystems, since they too undergo photosynthesis and serve as a vital food source for other organisms.

Plants play a crucial role in the nutrient cycles of ecosystems. They take in carbon dioxide from the air during photosynthesis and use it to build their own tissues. When vegetation is eaten, this organic carbon is used to build animal tissue and as a source of energy. The carbon is converted into carbon dioxide and released back into the air through respiration, the decay of animal

ECOSYSTEMS

An ecosystem consists of a community of living things and its physical environment. Terrestrial ecosystems include forest, savanna, grassland, scrubland, tundra, and desert. Marine and freshwater aquatic ecosystems include oceans, lakes, rivers, and wetlands. Ecosystems are categorized into abiotic components—minerals, climate, soil, water, sunlight—and biotic components—all living members and associated entities such as carcasses and wastes.

wastes, and the decomposition of tissues after the animal's death. This exchange is called the carbon cycle.

Plants are also involved in mineral cycles. For example, plants get nitrogen compounds from the soil and combine them with carbohydrates to make proteins. Animals get the nitrogen compounds they need by eating plant proteins. The nitrogen returns to the soil as animal waste. Bacteria and fungi then turn the waste back into simple nitrogen compounds, which the plants can use once more.

PLANTS AND THE DEVELOPMENT OF ECOSYSTEMS

Ecosystems, like organisms, are born, develop, and mature. Disturbances, such as volcanic eruptions, fires, or windstorms, create new habitats and start a process of ecosystem development called succession. Plants play a significant role in succession.

Marram grass establishes a beachhead of sorts on the dunes of Cape Cod, Mass. Plants can change the surrounding environment through their role in a process known as succession. Shutterstock.com

The succession of ecosystems on sand dunes near the Great Lakes has been intensively studied by ecologists. Over the past 10,000 years, the water level of the Great Lakes has been slowly dropping. As this happens, living things gradually become established on sand dunes surrounding the lakes. Initially, sand dunes are a very inhospitable environment, and only the most hardy plants can grow there. The roots of these pioneer plants stabilize the sand, however, making it possible for other species to move onto the dunes.

Eventually a dense growth of marram grass covers the dune. This grass produces an extensive root system that holds the dune in place, and organic matter from the grass's decaying roots and stems increases the fertility of the soil. This makes the environment more favorable for the growth of shrubs and pines. As the shrubs and pines grow, their shade slowly kills the marram grass, which is replaced with a dense pine forest.

The pines do not reproduce in their own shade, but they create a habitat suitable for the establishment of broad-leaved trees such as oaks, maples, and elms. Thus, the pines are gradually replaced by these deciduous broad-leaved trees, which can reproduce in the forest environment. Once established,

this type of forest will not change into another type of ecosystem. This final form is called the climax. The entire process of ecosystem succession may take hundreds of years. The series of stages, from the pioneer to the climax, that make up a succession is called a sere, and each stage is called a seral stage.

Such successional patterns may occur on bare rock after glaciation or volcanic eruption, or in fields abandoned by farmers. Succession also occurs around the margins of small lakes. Here, such plants as sedges and cattails, which can tolerate the constant presence of water, grow along the lake's margins. Sediment and debris from these plants accumulate, gradually filling the lake from its edges. Other species less tolerant of water can then become established.

During succession the number of plant species gradually increases. Consequently the total amount of plant tissue produced each year also increases. This makes the environment hospitable for more animal species. As a result, as succession progresses, ecosystems tend to become more complex.

Debris from cattails and other vegetation gradually creates a mat of sediment that supports the growth of other plants that are not so tolerant of a lakeshore's watery environment. **Shutterstock.com**

Plant succession is a major means by which ecosystems repair themselves after a disturbance. After a wildfire, for example, certain species of plants grow very quickly. Their rapid growth minimizes soil erosion and allows other plants to become established. In ecosystems such as the chaparral of the southwestern United States, the seeds of many of these pioneer plants lie dormant in the soil. The heat of a fire stimulates them to germinate. They grow quickly, produce dormant seeds, die, and are not seen again until the next fire.

COMPETITION AND COOPERATION

Interactions between plants affect their distribution and abundance. When a major resource, such as water or nitrogen, is in short supply, plants may compete with each other for use of the resource. Species that can use the resource more effectively are likely to grow faster and therefore to be more abundant. Such competition affects plant succession. Competition is also apparent in such ecosystems as agricultural fields. Many weeds are better able to use water and minerals than are the crop plants with which they

The pallor of Indian pipe is a prime indication that the plant does not produce chlorophyll. Therefore, in order to get nutrients, Indian pipe must feed off a host plant. **Gerry Bishop/Visuals Unlimited/ Getty Images**

grow. Consequently, farmers must employ various methods of weed control to check the spread of weeds.

Some plants depend entirely on competition for their survival. The strangler fig, which grows in the tropics, provides an

Spanish moss drapes the limbs of a tree. Epiphytes such as these root on a host tree but get water and minerals on their own. Shutterstock.com

excellent example. Birds carry its seeds to the branches of a host tree. Here the seeds germinate and send down roots that surround the host tree. The fig produces abundant branches and leaves that eventually rob the host tree of sunlight. The host tree dies, and the mature fig tree is left standing alone.

Some plants produce roots that invade the tissues of a host plant. Parasites such as mistletoe, which are capable of photosynthesis, obtain only water and minerals from their host. Others, like the Indian pipe and pine drops, produce no chlorophyll and depend entirely on food drawn from their host.

Some plants compete by producing chemicals that are toxic to other plants. For example, very few plants can grow beneath a walnut tree, because organic chemicals produced by the tree prevent or stunt the growth

Not all interactions between plants are destructive. Some plants provide habitats for other plants. In wet tropical zones, for example, the branches of trees support plants called epiphytes, or air plants. These plants are not parasites; they draw neither food nor water from the plants to which they cling. Their roots serve merely to hold them on the host tree, and the plants obtain moisture and minerals from rainwater. The Spanish moss

that grows in the southeastern United States is an epiphyte. (It is actually not a moss at all, but a distant relative of the pineapple.)

PLANTS OF EXTREME HABITATS

Plants that are able to survive hot, dry climates are called xerophytes. Xerophytes have a wide variety of adaptations to conserve water. For example, most plants that grow in deserts have thick waxy cuticles on the outer surfaces of their leaves to minimize water loss. In many desert plants, such as cacti, leaves may be absent altogether. In such plants photosynthesis is carried out in the outer tissues of the thick, fleshy stems. Many cacti have extensive shallow roots. When it rains, these roots can take up large quantities of water very quickly. This water is stored in the central core of the stems. Cacti can survive in the desert for years on the water gathered from a single rainfall.

Some desert plants survive desert drought by becoming dormant. The ocotillo of the southwestern United States and Mexico resembles a bunch of dead sticks most of the time. Following a rain, however, it quickly produces leaves that begin making food. Within a few weeks, the plant produces

A blooming water lily. Plants such as these, called hydrophytes, are perfectly at home is excessively wet locations such as pond banks—or ponds themselves. Shutterstock.com

flowers. When its seeds mature, the ocotillo loses its leaves and becomes dormant again.

Many annual desert plants germinate only after heavy rain. They quickly grow, flower, and produce seeds. The parent plant then dies and the seeds are deposited in the soil. These seeds are very resistant to heat and

drought and remain dormant in the soil until the next heavy rain.

Many plants cannot survive in habitats that have a great deal of water. When the soil is saturated with water, oxygen is unavailable to plant roots. Plants that grow in very wet habitats are called hydrophytes. They often have spongy stem tissue containing air channels that extend down into the roots. Oxygen produced during photosynthesis and taken from the air is transported down these channels to the roots. The roots of many hydrophytes are also able to respire anaerobically, or without oxygen.

Plants that grow in the Arctic or on high mountain slopes must be able to endure severe cold and very short growing seasons. These plants have specialized cell structures that prevent damage from ice-crystal formation. In addition, many of these species are able to carry out life processes at unusually cold temperatures. Many Arctic grasses, for example, photosynthesize best at temperatures very near the freezing point.

Nitrogen-Fixing Plants

Of all the mineral nutrients in the soil, nitrogen is generally the most difficult for plants to acquire. Even though nitrogen is the most abundant element in the air, most organisms are unable to obtain the nitrogen they need from the air. Most plants depend on mineral forms of nitrogen in the soil, and land animals ultimately depend on organic nitrogen produced by plants.

Nitrogen-fixing plants are able to take atmospheric nitrogen directly into their roots because of an alliance they have with certain bacteria. These bacteria are found in specialized nodules on the plants' roots. The bacteria take nitrogen gas from the air, convert it to organic forms of nitrogen, and make it available to their host plant. In return, the host plant provides the bacteria with food that they are unable to manufacture for themselves. This is an example of one of the many forms of mutualism, or mutually beneficial partnerships found in nature.

Nitrogen-fixing plants include members of the legume family (peas, beans, and their relatives), alders, and other shrubs. Many of these plants are significant sources of protein in the human diet. Some also play a part in succession. For example, nitrogen-fixing shrubs grow in soils formed from volcanic lavas. They enrich the soil with nitrogen, making it possible for other species to establish themselves.

Insect-Eating Plants

A number of plants are capable of eating small animals, especially insects. These plants are called insectivorous plants. Examples include the Venus's-flytrap, pitcher plants, sundews, and bladderworts. These unusual plants are most often found in moist and nutrient-poor habitats, such as bogs. The insects that the plants trap are not a major source of organic food—rather, they provide mineral nutrients such as nitrogen and phosphorus in these infertile habitats.

Insectivorous plants employ a variety of mechanisms to catch their prey. The sundew has sticky glands located on the ends of hairs on its leaves. Insects become stuck and eventually entangled in these hairs and are then digested by chemicals released from the leaf. Pitcher plants have tubular leaves that produce chemicals attractive to insects. Once the insect has crawled inside the leaf, it is unable to escape. The Venus's-flytrap has perhaps the most elaborate mechanism for catching insects. Its leaves form a snap-trap that is triggered when an insect touches hairs on the leaf's surface. The leaf quickly folds around and traps the insect.

THE VENUS'S-FLYTRAP

One of the best known of the insect-eating plants is the Venus's-flytrap, a perennial of the sundew family. At the end of each leaf it has a pair of hinged lobes, or jaws, edged with spines. When an insect or other small animal alights on a lobe, the jaws fold together and trap it.

The "jaws" of a Venus's-flytrap, probably the most familiar insect-eating plant. Shutterstock.com

This small plant is found in the wild only in eastern North and South Carolina, where it is common in damp, mossy areas. The plant bears a round cluster of small white flowers at the tip of an erect stem that grows from 8 to 12 inches (20 to 30 cm) tall. The leaves are 3 to 5 inches (8 to 13 cm) long and form a rosette. Each leaf ends in two lobes that form a trap. Crimson glands give the lobes a red, flowerlike appearance to attract insects. The plant's traps are "set" only when the Sun shines.

On the surface of each lobe are three highly sensitive hairs. In normal daytime temperatures, when these hairs are stimulated by an insect or by any other means, the lobes snap shut in about half a second. The spines along the edges interlock to hold fast the captive, and the glands on the lobes' surface secrete an acidic fluid that digests the insect's body. About 10 days are required for digestion, and then the leaf reopens. A leaf rarely captures more than three insects in its lifetime.

HOW PLANTS PASS THE WINTER

In summer, plants make and store food in their roots, stems, or seeds. In winter, they rest. Plants pass the winter in various ways.

ANNUALS

Annuals flower in the same season that they are planted. Then, transferring all their reserve food to their seeds, the plants wither and die. Inside the protective seed covering, the embryonic plant lies dormant until the moisture and warmth of spring stimulate its growth.

BIENNIALS

Biennials form only leaves and buds during the first season and store food in their underground roots. The upper parts die in the winter. During the following season the reserve food from the roots is used to make new stems, which bear flowers and seeds. In the second winter the plants die. Their seeds produce a new generation in the spring. Examples of such plants include beets, turnips, parsnips, carrots, and many common flowers.

Many biennial plants lose their stems and upper leaves in the winter but keep their green basal leaves. The leaves grow in beautifully patterned rosettes. They lie flat on the ground, spread out around an underground

The leafy rosette of a young common mullein plant, a biennial herb that can grow to 10 feet (3 meters) in height. Shutterstock.com

taproot. The function of such rosettes may be to supply the root with water. The leaves are slightly grooved, and rainwater pours from the outside and top of the cluster to the center and so down to the root.

PERENNIALS

Perennials go on living from year to year. In cold climates they store food in their roots or stems and rest during the winter. In warm climates they simply continue growing. Trees and shrubs are typical perennials. They shed their leaves and for the winter form an insulating jacket of waxy scales on the buds from which new growth will appear the next year.

As the days grow shorter and the nights grow longer and colder, the food substances stored in the leaves of perennial plants flow back into the twigs, branches, and trunk. The gradual decrease in temperature causes changes in the plant tissues that make them more resistant to cold. This preparation for the upcoming winter months is called hardening. When the chlorophyll decomposes chemically and becomes colorless, the leaves take on their autumn colors of yellow, red, and orange. These colors are caused by the

Pigments other than chlorophyll give a maple leaf its autumn colors.
© **Corbis**

presence of pigments other than chlorophyll. Many of them are always present, but during the summer there is so much more chlorophyll that these colors are masked.

While these color changes occur, a thick, corky skin called an abscission, or separation, layer grows between the stem of the leaf and the branch. After this layer has formed, it splits in two. Half of the layer goes with the leaf when it drops off; the other half covers the scar on the branch and seals the tissues against insects and moisture loss. Oak leaves fall very late in the year because the abscission layers are not perfectly formed earlier in the season. In tropical ecosystems, where there is a change from wet to dry seasons, many trees drop their leaves during the dry season. This prevents the trees from losing moisture through evaporation from the leaves.

The winter study of twigs can be quite instructive. It is possible to identify trees and shrubs by their twigs alone, for no two kinds of twigs have exactly the same arrangement of buds and leaf scars. The buds are tiny, living plant parts that develop into leaves or flower clusters. They are covered with overlapping, waxy bud scales. At the top of the stem is the terminal bud. The stem grows in length from the terminal bud. This bud may or may not

produce flowers. New branches grow from the side buds.

Bud scales are modified leaves. In the spring, as they expand in response to the warmth and rain, they may take on soft colors, such as the yellow and rose of the hickory and horse chestnut scales. The scales of sumac do not fall off but develop into true leaves. The colored "petals" of the flowering dogwood are actually the expanded scales of the bud. The true flower is a small cluster inside this leaf, which is called a bract.

The flowering dogwood, a North American species, is widely grown as an ornamental for its showy petallike bracts (modified leaves) under the tiny flowers. © Epantha/Fotolia

CONCLUSION

Every year in cold climates, the emergence of green sprouts from the soil is a sure sign that spring is on its way. Because this process happens naturally, without our help, it is easy to take for granted. In reality, however, the development of a plant from a seed to a sprout to a fully grown specimen—be it a redwood, a rosebush, or even just a weed—involves a complex series of processes such as respiration and photosynthesis. Similarly, the ability of a plant to thrive depends on a number of interacting factors, including environmental elements such as the availability of sunlight and water, the plant's adaptations to its environment, and its relationship to other living things in its ecosystem.

As sources of food and oxygen, plants are vital parts of nearly all terrestrial ecosystems and play an indispensable role in the existence in life on Earth. Thus their reproduction and subsequent growth remain subjects of vital importance and interest to people everywhere.

abscission The natural separation of flowers, fruit, or leaves from plants at a special separation layer.

cambium A thin layer of vascular-plant tissue that continuously generates new cells and is responsible for secondary plant growth.

cellulose A complex carbohydrate that is the main component of plant cell walls.

chlorophyll Any member of the most important class of pigments involved in photosynthesis.

chloroplast Structure within a green plant cell in which photosynthesis occurs.

cotyledon The first leaf, or one of the first pair or whorl of leaves, developed by the embryo of a seed plant.

cytoplasm The jellylike substance inside a cell that is made up of water, proteins, and other molecules.

endosperm A food-containing tissue in seed plants that nourishes the embryo.

epiphyte A plant that gets moisture and minerals from the air and rain and that usually grows on another plant.

gamete A mature sex cell that is capable of uniting with a gamete of the opposite sex to begin the formation of a new individual.

gametophyte The structure in certain plants that produces gametes for the sexual phase of the alternation of generations.

gemma An asexual reproductive body that becomes detached from the parent plant and can develop into a new plant.

germination The sprouting of a seed, spore, or other reproductive body.

meiosis The process by which a gamete, or sex cell, divides; the resulting cells have half the number of chromosomes.

photosynthesis The process by which green plants transform light energy into chemical energy.

pistil Female reproductive part of a flower.

sere A series of ecological communities formed in ecological succession.

sporophyte The structure in certain plants that produces spores for the nonsexual phase of the alternation of generations.

stamen Male reproductive part of a flower.

stigma The upper part of the pistil of a flower that receives the pollen grains and on which they start to grow.

stolon A stem that grows erect from the base of a plant and then curves over, touching the ground at the tip. It produces new plants from buds at its tip or nodes.

stoma A tiny opening or pore in the top layer of a leaf or young stem.

transpiration A plant's loss of water, mainly through the stomata of leaves.

tropisms Growth patterns wherein plants turn or grow toward or away from a stimulus such as light (the Sun) or moisture.

turgor Water pressure within a cell, which makes living plant tissue rigid.

xerophyte A plant that grows well in dry conditions.

FOR MORE INFORMATION

Botanical Research Institute of Texas
1700 University Drive
Fort Worth, Texas 76107
(817) 332-4441
Web site: http://www.brit.org
The Botanical Research Institute of Texas
is dedicated to increasing public under-
standing of plants through its research
projects, extensive library of publications, and educational programs.

Botanical Society of America
4475 Castleman Avenue
St. Louis, MO 63110
(314) 577-9566
Web site: http://www.botany.org
The Botanical Society of America is a clear-
inghouse of research on plants and related
organisms, conducted by professionals,
academics, and educators in the botanical
field. The organization also offers publications and outreach programs.

Center for Plant Conservation
PO Box 299
St. Louis, MO 63166
(314) 577-9450
Web site: http://www.centerforplant
conservation.org

The Center for Plant Conservation is made up of more than 30 botanical institutions that are dedicated to conserving plants native to the United States through research and restoration efforts.

Native Plant Society of British Columbia (NPSBC)
1917 West 4th Avenue, Suite 195
Vancouver, BC V6J 1M7
Canada
(604) 831-5069
Web site: http://www.npsbc.org
The NPSBC is centered on the study of plants native to British Columbia. Member events include field trips, workshops, and presentations by guest speakers.

Torrey Botanical Society
PO Box 7065
Lawrence, KS 66044
(800) 627-0326
Web site: http://www.torreybotanical.org
Established in 1867, the Torrey Botanical Society encourages interest in botany through professional publications, lectures, and hands-on field trips in the New York tri-state area.

University of British Columbia Botanical
  Garden and Centre for Plant Research
6804 SW Marine Drive
Vancouver, BC V6T 1Z4
Canada
(604) 822-3928
Web site: http://www.ubcbotanicalgarden.org
The living plant collection at the UBC
  Botanical Garden provides researchers at
  its associated Centre for Plant Research
  with material for their world-class
  studies in such areas as evolution and
  biodiversity.

WEB SITES

Due to the changing nature of Internet links,
Rosen Educational Services has developed an
online list of Web sites related to the subject
of this book. This site is updated regularly.
Please use this link to access the list:

http://www.rosenlinks.com/biol/prge

Angier, Bradford. *Field Guide to Medicinal Wild Plants* (Stackpole, 2000).

Baker, Margaret. *Discovering the Folklore of Plants*, 3rd ed. (Shire, 1996).

Barbour, M.G., and others. *Terrestrial Plant Ecology*, 3rd ed. (Benjamin Cummings, 1999).

Bold, H.C., and others. *Morphology of Plants and Fungi*, 5th ed. (Harper, 1987).

Cork, Barbara. *Mysteries and Marvels of Plant Life* (EDC, 1989).

Dowden, A.O. *From Flower to Fruit* (Ticknor & Fields, 1994).

Elliott, Douglas. *Wild Roots* (Healing Arts, 1995).

Freethy, Ron. *From Agar to Zenry: A Book of Plant Uses, Names and Folklore* (Longwood, 1985).

Howell, Laura, and others. *World of Plants* (Scholastic, 2003).

Huxley, Anthony. *Green Inheritance: The WWF Book of Plants* (Univ. of Calif. Press, 2005).

Huxley, Anthony. *Plant and Planet* (Penguin, 1987).

Janulewicz, Mike. *Plants* (Gloucester Press, 1984).

Mabey, Richard. *Oak and Company* (Greenwillow, 1983).

Margulis, Lynn, and others. *Diversity of Life: The Illustrated Guide to the Five Kingdoms* (Jones and Bartlett, 1999).

Pringle, Laurence. *Being a Plant* (Crowell, 1983).

Rahn, J.E. *Plants That Changed History; More Plants That Changed History* (Macmillan, 1982; 1985).

Raven, P.H., and others. *Biology of Plants*, 7th ed. (Freeman, 2005).

Salisbury, F.B., and Ross, C.W. *Plant Physiology*, 4th ed. (Wadsworth, 1992).

Selsam, M.E. *The Plants We Eat*, rev. ed. (Morrow, 1981).

Scott, Jane. *Botany in the Field: An Introduction to Plant Communities for the Amateur Naturalist* (Prentice, 1984).

Spellenberg, Richard. *National Audubon Society Field Guide to North American Wildflowers: Western Region* (Knopf, 2004).

Thieret, J.W., and others. *National Audubon Society Field Guide to North American Wildflowers: Eastern Region* (Knopf, 2004).